INSIDE INDIA

AMAZING HISTORICAL PLACES

Written by
Shachii Manik

Illustrated & designed by
Ahmed Sikander

HarperCollins*Children's Books*

Created by Fun OK PLease Content Publishing Pvt. Ltd

First published in India in 2018 by HarperCollins *Children's Books*
An imprint of HarperCollins *Publishers*
A-75, Sector 57, Noida, Uttar Pradesh 201301, India
www.harpercollins.co.in

2 4 6 8 10 9 7 5 3 1

Copyright Text © Shachii Manik 2018
Copyright Visuals © Ahmed Sikander

P-ISBN: 9 7 8 - 9 3 - 5 2 7 7 - 7 4 6 - 4

Shachii Manik asserts the moral right to be identified as the
author of the work.

Typeset in Atma Serif (11.5/16) and Brandson Grotesque (11/16)

Acknowledgements:

The creators of this book would like to acknowledge the efforts of our
young interns, Ms Tanvi Shah and Ms Aadhya Shivakumar, for their
invaluable efforts in collating and putting together the research material
that allowed the creation of this unique book.

Conceptualised & Created by:

FunOKPlease Content Publishing Pvt. Ltd
Mumbai - 400 016
Visit us at www.funokplease.com
Send us your feedback to: admin@funokplease.com

Printed and bound at Replika Press Pvt. Ltd.

How to use this book:

Hi, I'm Indy and this is my friend, Dia. We're about to take you on a whirlwind tour of glorious India. As you travel through the pages of this book and do all the fun activities, you will learn about the various historical places in our country, some well-known and some that you will come across for the first time. We have had an amazing time trekking around the country and collecting all these clever and amusing things to do, and we hope that you enjoy them too.

A few things you should know before you begin your journey:

1. It is extremely dangerous to try these activities while standing on your head or even on one foot. **Believe us, we've tried!**

2. Most of the activities are best done with a pencil. **So that you can erase and do them over and over again!** Look for .

3. Some of the activities are spread over two non-consecutive **not side-by-side** pages. Look for matching symbols on the pages to find their pairs. Such as:

4. Have an adult supervise your cooking experiences and craft projects. **Beware! Fire is hot and scissors are sharp!**

5. Some of the activities have solutions given on the last few pages of the book. **Don't even try sneaking a peek at them before you've tried solving them yourself!**

Have fun!

WHAT'S INSIDE?

Cool Activities

Word Games
Quizzes
Recipes
Design Your Own Clock Tower
Make Your Own Story
Create Your Own Flag
Word Searches
Search and Find
Number Games
Spot the Differences
Craft
Two-Player Games

Historical Places

Forts of Rajasthan
Caves of Bhimbetka
Hero Stones
Harappan Digs
Jantar Mantar
Clock Towers
Churches
Pillars
Temples of Maluti
Stepwells
Qutb Minar
Golconda Fort
Brihadeshwara Temple
Bahubali
Ashoka's Edicts
Temple Vaults
And much more ...

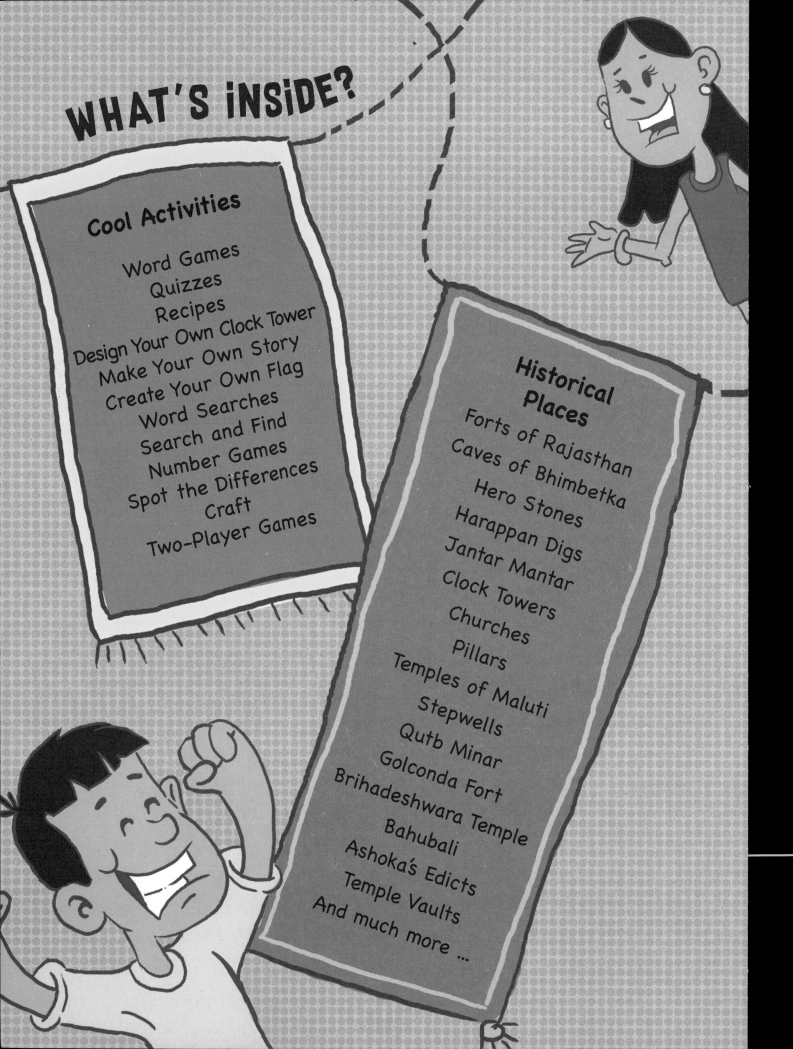

CAMOUFLAGED FORTS

A fort is a defensive structure built to protect a city or its troops. India has seen the rise and fall of thousands of forts in its rich history. Hidden carefully in this jumble of letters, away from the enemy's eyes, are some of the forts that Dia visited during her trip around the country. She has challenged Indy to find all 16 in the grid. Can you help him?

D	P	A	I	C	N	N	A	Q	B	Z	H	V	A	Y	B	U	O	M	I
R	H	V	J	Z	S	D	K	I	A	D	N	O	C	L	O	G	X	C	P
E	Y	L	A	L	Q	I	L	A	R	L	X	A	W	I	N	V	F	M	J
Q	A	P	T	G	Y	A	R	O	M	V	D	K	F	C	Z	H	A	E	Q
L	O	X	G	E	U	K	E	M	N	E	X	E	L	U	Q	U	T	H	I
A	I	U	C	R	B	A	Z	C	G	Z	R	O	K	B	I	D	A	R	Z
M	R	G	H	L	S	T	D	H	Y	D	J	W	R	S	L	X	N	A	C
A	K	W	I	X	B	P	Z	A	B	T	F	E	H	D	A	B	Q	N	E
M	I	N	T	R	A	I	G	A	D	H	M	Y	G	Y	M	W	Y	G	R
E	S	A	T	A	V	T	O	K	I	L	R	P	A	C	U	R	A	A	T
U	R	K	O	Z	F	I	A	Y	A	S	A	O	P	Z	B	D	E	R	D
O	U	H	R	D	A	Q	Z	S	P	K	C	W	I	N	A	T	A	H	K
Q	P	A	G	H	O	D	I	W	I	E	U	N	L	L	R	V	S	H	O
B	H	S	A	R	N	A	G	A	R	D	H	A	N	I	A	B	I	P	F
Y	E	F	R	O	J	Y	N	Z	I	O	B	Z	F	Y	K	W	R	Y	A
G	T	X	H	Q	V	T	E	J	A	S	C	Q	I	D	W	U	G	L	M
M	A	D	L	M	B	O	D	Y	R	G	L	A	P	Y	O	B	A	R	J
W	F	Y	A	O	I	H	D	A	G	L	A	B	M	U	K	X	R	H	V
C	H	N	T	K	C	S	K	V	A	E	P	O	X	N	L	F	H	Z	C
F	R	M	U	R	U	D	J	A	N	J	I	R	A	P	C	S	W	L	E

Forts

Aguada	Murud Janjira	Kumbhalgarh	Qila Mubarak
Chittorgarh	Amer	Nagardhan	Bidar
Jaisalmer	Fatehpur Sikri	Lal Qila	Gwalior
Mehrangarh	Raigad	Asirgarh	Golconda

BRiGHTEN UP THE WALLS

If you travel about 45 km northeast of Bhopal, Madhya Pradesh, you can visit a 15,000-year-old art gallery! The cave paintings of Bhimbetka are one of the oldest known works of art. They give us a peek into the lives of the ancient cave people.

It's obvious that they did not have watercolours, acrylic or oil paints. Then what did they use to make these paintings?

Here are some simple ways to make basic colours from things you can find in your kitchen. Try them out and then brighten up the brown page with a cave painting of your own.

YELLOW: Turmeric powder + hot water. Let it cool. Add just enough water so that the paste is neither too thick nor too runny.

TERRACOTTA (brown orange): Kashmiri red chilli powder + hot water.

BROWN: Black coffee + hot water.

LIGHT BROWN: Tea bags + hot water.

GREEN: Spinach or fenugreek leaves + few spoons of water. Blend into a paste.

PINK: Beetroot juice.

ORANGE: Marigold flowers + water. Grind.

RED: Kumkum powder + water.

GREY: Coal + water.

BLACK: This is the most interesting one. Burn a diya (oil / ghee lamp). Cover it with a bowl or an empty clay diya. The cover will collect black soot. Mix this soot with oil to make a brilliant black paste.

DIGGING IN THE DIRT

Help Prof. Banerjee dig up treasure hidden in the ruins of Harappa. Open page 11 and play with a friend. Secretly mark an X on one of your squares. Your opponent must guess where your X is. Take turns asking questions such as: 'A5?', 'Is it south of the river?', 'Is it under a tree?' The first one to locate the opponent's X wins!

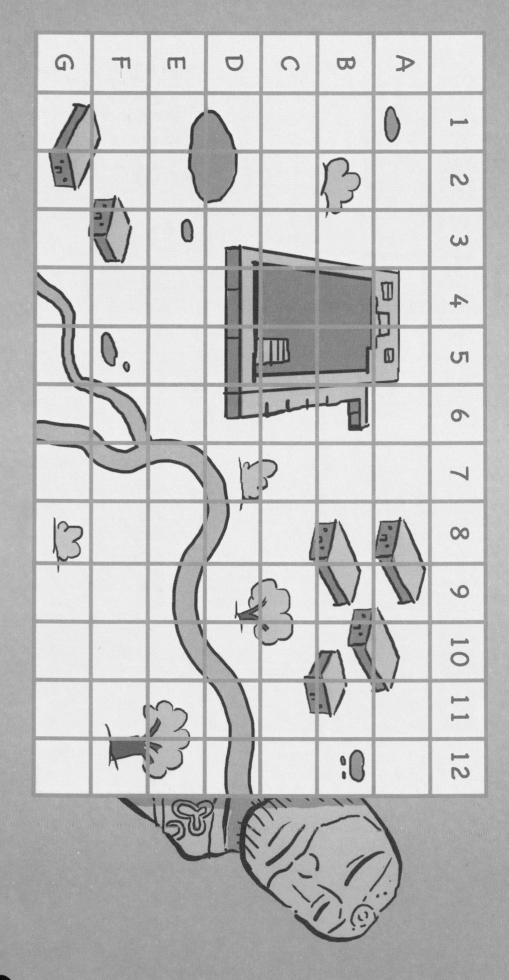

DESIGN YOUR ENSIGN

Most forts used to have a flag fluttering proudly from their ramparts. The flags would represent the rulers and their values. Our Indian tricolour today adorns the Red Fort and represents what our nation stands for.

Imagine you were the ruler of your very own kingdom. Design a flag that would stand atop your fort.

iT'S NOT YOUR VAULT!

Sree Padmanabhaswamy Temple in Thiruvananthapuram, Kerala, is known to be the richest temple in the world. It is uncertain when the temple was built, but it has been mentioned in historical texts from as far back as the 9th century CE. The temple has six vaults (A to F). Vaults A, C, D, E and F have been opened in the past and crores of rupees worth of gold, diamonds and precious stones have been found. Legend has it that the mysterious Vault B has never been opened and that if it ever is, it will spell doom for whoever opens it.

On Indy's first day at school this year, his teacher handed him a sheet of paper containing the code needed to open his locker. Can you help him decode it?

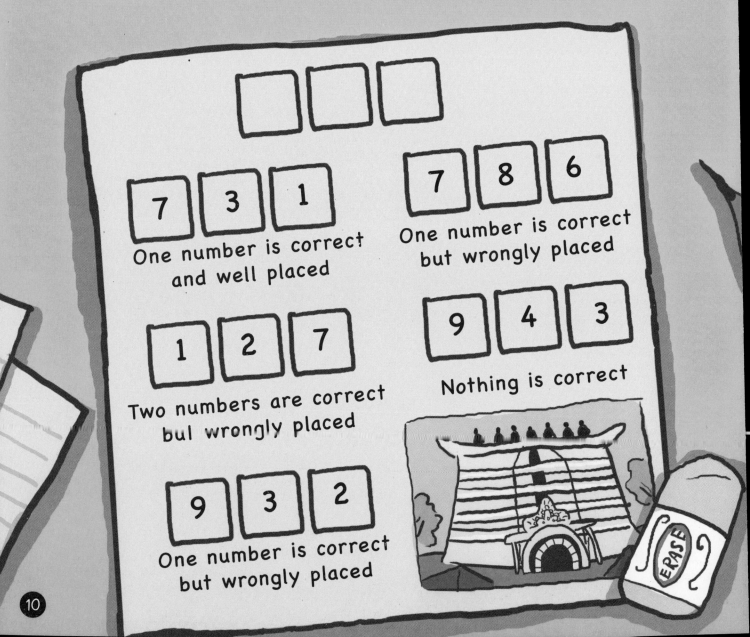

One number is correct and well placed

One number is correct but wrongly placed

Two numbers are correct but wrongly placed

Nothing is correct

One number is correct but wrongly placed

LOOK FOR

DIGGING IN THE DIRT

Help Prof. Banerjee dig up treasure hidden in the ruins of Harappa. Open page 8 and play with a friend. Secretly mark an X on one of your squares. Your opponent must guess where your X is. Take turns asking questions such as: 'A5?', 'Is it south of the river?', 'Is it under a tree?' The first one to locate the opponent's X wins!

11

TASTY TREATS FOR TOOTHLESS TYCOONS

Legend has it that the famous melt-in-the-mouth Galouti Kebab was created by a royal chef for the Nawab of Awadh, Asaf-ud-Daulah, in the 16th century. He was really fond of kebabs (like most of us!) and his khansamas (royal chefs) took delight in creating new and fancy (yet chewy) kebabs for him every day. But as he grew old, he lost his teeth and couldn't chew on the normal kebabs. So his chef specially created the Galouti ('soft') Kebab for him, which needed minimum chewing but was bursting with flavour. Apparently, it needs more than 150 spices to get the flavour just right. Because the Nawab was extremely generous, the workers toiling away at building the Bada Imambara got a chance to try these kebabs as well. Have we got your mouth watering? Let's make our own delicious Paneer Galouti Kebabs.

Ingredients

Whip out your box of 150 spices … Just kidding! Ha ha!
Ingredients that we will use:
1 large potato, boiled and mashed
1 cup boiled sweet corn, crushed
100 gm paneer (crumbled). Use very soft paneer. Fresh paneer, homemade or from a dairy (not the packaged, processed kind), works best.
1/2 cup breadcrumbs or soaked poha
1 tsp ginger and green chilli paste
1/4 tsp garam masala
1/4 tsp turmeric
1/4 tsp coriander-cumin powder
1 tsp cornflour
Few drops of lemon juice or 1 tbsp curd
Salt to taste

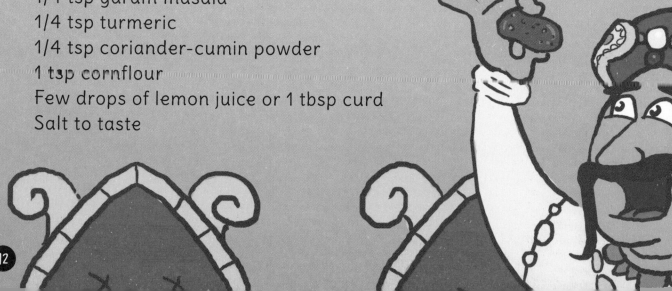

Method

1. In a large bowl, combine all the ingredients to make a kebab mixture.
2. Divide the mixture into small balls (like ping-pong balls). Refrain from tossing them in the air!
3. Flatten each ball to form a kebab. Refrigerate for 30 mins.
4. Heat oil in a frying pan and shallow fry the kebabs on both sides until golden.
5. Take them off the heat. These delicious royal kebabs are best enjoyed with a yummy coriander-mint chutney or any sauce of your choice (and also, all your teeth in place).

Make sure that there are trumpets playing with a royal flourish as you serve them.

MAKE THE RIGHT CHOICE

1. Which city has the famous chariot-shaped temple dedicated to the Sun God, built in the 13th century by King Narsimhadeva 1 of the Eastern Ganga Dynasty?
   a) Puri (—)
   b) Kolkata (—)
   c) Lucknow (—)
   d) Konark (—)

2. This famous tomb made of white marble stands majestically along the banks of the Yamuna River.
   a) Humayun's Tomb (—)
   b) Taj Mahal (—)
   c) Haji Ali Dargah (—)
   d) Bibi ka Maqbara (—)

3. The Great Stupa at Sanchi was built in the 3rd century BCE and is said to contain relics of Lord Buddha. Which great king commissioned the building of this and other stupas?
   a) Emperor Ashoka (—)
   b) Chandragupta Maurya (—)
   c) Raja Raja Chola (—)
   d) King Samudragupta (—)

4. The Buland Darwaza was built in the year 1601 by Emperor Akbar to commemorate his victory over Gujarat. You can climb its 42 steps and walk under the archway into a large courtyard. Where is this lofty gateway located?
   a) Ahmedabad (—)
   b) New Delhi (—)
   c) Hyderabad (—)
   d) Fatehpur Sikri (—)

5. The Palace of Winds was built by Maharaja Sawai Pratap in the Pink City of Jaipur, Rajasthan, in 1799. It is a fine example of Rajput architecture with its delicately carved windows, behind which the royal women would sit to enjoy the events and festivals on the street. What is this popular palace better known as?
   a) Jai Mahal   (—)
   b) Vayu Vihar   (—)
   c) Hawa Mahal   (—)
   d) Jal Vihar   (—)

6. This monument, the tomb of Mohammed Adil Shah, stands 47.5 m tall in the town of Bijapur, Karnataka. It was built between 1626 and 1656, and its name literally means 'circular dome'.
   a) Dodda Gummata   (—)
   b) Gol Matol   (—)
   c) Gol Gumbaz   (—)
   d) Gol Gubbara   (—)

7. On which island can you find the famous Cellular Jail or Kala Pani, one of the most dreaded and gruelling colonial prisons, built in 1906?
   a) Andaman and Nicobar   (—)
   b) Lakshadweep   (—)
   c) Elephanta   (—)
   d) Jambudwip   (—)

8. The Iconic Charminar was built in 1591 by Muhammed Quli Qutb Shah. Its imposing structure with a square base and four minarets has become a symbol of Hyderabad. Why was it built?
   a) To commemorate his victory in war   (—)
   b) To serve as a backdrop for
      a literature festival   (—)
   c) To mark the end of the plague   (—)
   d) To establish his capital there   (—)

PiLLARS, PiLLARS EVERYWHERE!

The Meenakshi Amman temple complex in Madurai, Tamil Nadu is a city temple. It houses 14 magnificent Gopurams (towers), including two golden Gopurams for the main deities that have been elaborately sculptured and painted. The twin temples of Lord Shiva and Goddess Meenakshi are almost nine storeys high. The origin of this temple can be traced back to the 14th century.

A highlight of this temple is the Hall of Thousand Pillars (there are 985 actually!). No matter where you look from, the pillars always appear to form perfect rows and columns. Here's a puzzle: Which set of instructions below was used to draw this shape around the pillars? Circle the starting dot.

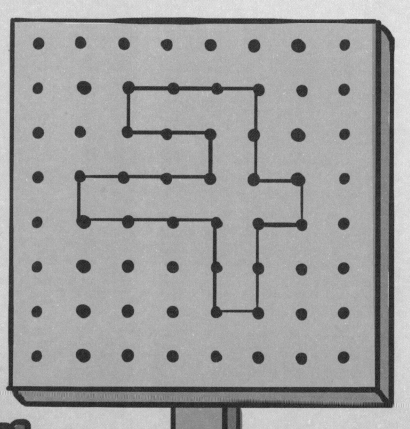

1. East 3, south 2, east 1, south 1, west 1, south 2, west 1, north 3, west 2, north 1, east 3, north 1, west 2, north 1, east 3, north 1, west 2, north 1

2. West 3, north 1, east 3, north 1, west 2, north 1, east 3, south 3, east 1, south 1, west 1, south 2, west 1, north 2

3. West 1, north 2, west 3, south 1, east 2, south 1, west 3, south 1, east 3, south 2, east 1, north 2, east 1, north 1

MAKE IT MEMORABLE!

First of all, DO NOT peek at page 31 (if you do, deadly invaders will attack the Kingdom of Vakatatka) before you complete this page. Nope, don't even think about it. Start by filling in all the blanks below, which will help you build your army and make it stronger! Then you can go to the mysterious page 31 and complete the story there, using all these words.

Tip: 🖐️ so that you can erase and create a brand new story.

A number between 900 and 1500 _____

A man's name _____

Adjective ending in -est _____   Adjective _____

Animal/bird _____   Adverb _____

Adverb _____   Noun _____

Family member _____   Abstract noun _____

Collective noun _____   A number greater than 1 _____

Plural noun _____   A number _____

Adjective _____   A happy exclamation _____

Adjective _____   Adjective _____

Family member _____   Verb ending in -ed _____

Profession _____

Noun _____

Verb _____

Bravo! Your army is all ready! It is now safe to head over to page 31 and fill in all the blanks in the story with these words.

BUILD IT!

Every historical place has a story to tell. But there are some stories brewing inside your head. Use some of the ideas that are shown here and build your own story about something that could have happened in history.

Characters:
- Horse
- Evil hairdresser
- Benevolent queen
- Eleven-year-old girl
- Trumpet player
- Marathon runner

Settings:
- Battlefield
- Kitchen
- Village marketplace
- Faraway island
- Dungeon

Events:
- Pouring rain
- A special shoe goes missing
- The sun does not rise on time
- Traffic jam
- A chase

Props:
- Chisel
- Crown
- Pencil
- Broom
- Diamond
- Arrow
- Wooden toy

You can use a maximum of three (and a minimum of one) categories from the list above to weave your tale.

_____

_____

_____

_____

_____

_____

_____

_____

RECREATE A WONDER

Tipu Sultan was a pioneer in the field of weapons. His creations shocked his enemies. Can you recreate one of his marvels here? Solve each expression to find out the sequence in which you need to connect the dots.

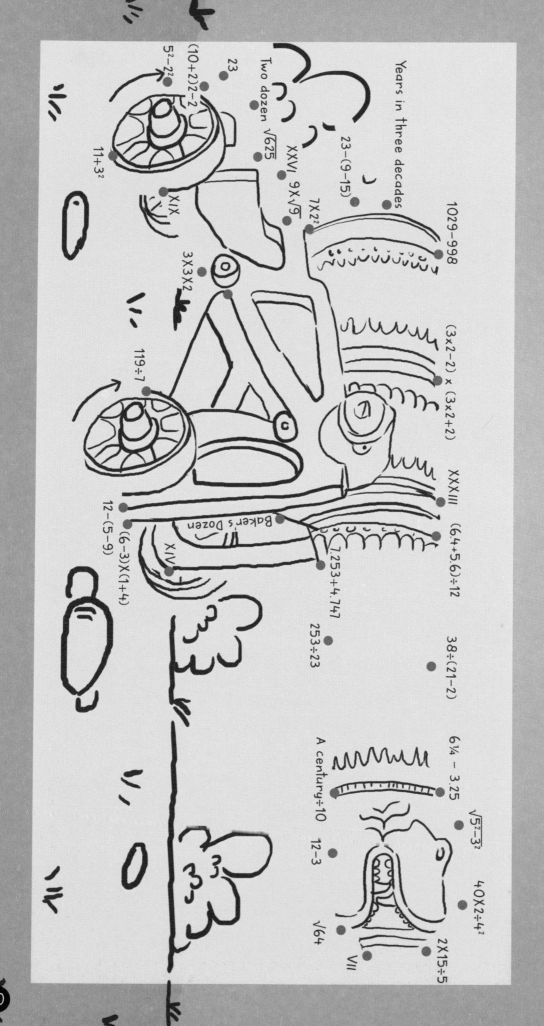

Years in three decades

1029−998

(3×2−2) × (3×2+2)

XXXIII

(64+5.6)÷12

38÷(21−2)

6¼ − 3.25

$\sqrt{5^2-3^2}$

4×2÷4²

2×15÷5

A century÷10

12−3

√64

VII

7.253+4.747

253÷23

Baker's Dozen

XIV

(6−3)×(1+4)

12−(5−9)

119÷7

3×3×2

XIX

7×2²

XXVI

9×√9

23−(9−15)

Two dozen

√625

23

(10+2)2−2

5²−2

11+3²

20

A STORY SET IN STONE

Imagine a comic strip dedicated to you. Now imagine it carved in stone! A 'hero stone' is a memorial created in honour of a brave person whose heroic deeds protected others from harm. Many such hero (and heroine, of course) stones have been discovered in various places around India. They date from anywhere between 3rd century BCE to 18th century CE. A typical hero stone is a flat, upright stone, 3–5 feet tall. It has three horizontal bands, with action scenes carved on each band. These scenes depict the story of the hero and his courageous deed.

Who is your hero or heroine? And why? Tell your story through your very own hero stone.

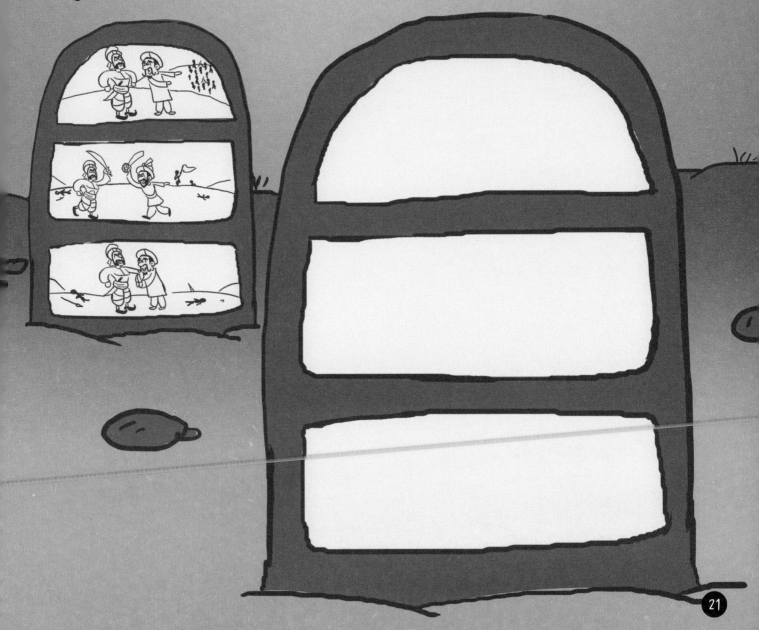

THiNK FAST

Can you think of all the following things beginning with a particular letter of the alphabet? Challenge your friend. Sit across from each other and hold the pages upright, so that your friend cannot see what you are writing.

Think of a letter of the alphabet (maybe it's the third letter of your first name). Set a timer for 3 minutes and begin writing.

Tip: so that you can erase and create a brand new story.

1. A monument _____

2. A king _____

3. A queen _____

4. A country that has been in a war _____

5. A food item _____

6. A part of a church _____

7. A fort in India _____

8. A city in India _____

9. A dance form _____

10. Material used in buildings _____

11. A type of vehicle _____

12. An old book _____

SCORE

Done? Now compare your answers with your friend's. If your answers in a category are unique, you get 2 points each. If your answers in a category are the same, you only get 1 point each. If you did not write anything for a particular category, you get no points for that, of course. Add up your points to see who wins!

Erase your answers and play again with another letter.

22

WHAT A VIEW!

Old palaces in Rajasthan are well known for their carved stone windows, called 'jaalis'. It is said that royal women would sit behind these brilliant pieces of intricate art and watch court proceedings. But if you thought these jaalis were made only because they look good … read on! There is science behind them. An average summer day in Rajasthan is mighty hot! Jaalis help in lowering the temperature by compressing the air through their many tiny holes.

Here's one such half-constructed carved window. Complete it and give it a sandstone-like finish!

THE PECULiAR PAMPHLET

Dia and Indy were visiting Maluti in the state of Jharkhand. While they were looking for information on the 72 temples of Maluti, they found this pamphlet lying on the floor. When they picked it up and began to read, something seemed wrong. Look at the pamphlet. Can you spot what is wrong?

Welcomme to the beeutiful villeage oft Maluti. You are amt the easteern end of the Chota Nagpur Plateau, aamong forestts, hillocks annd rivulets. Onjoy the frosh, cleann air in thiis sinple, peaceful, quitt envirenment, full of himstory. Make sure youp visit alll of the seeventy two terracotta templess that adorn oiur village. Thexe are tthe ones that remayn out off the 108 built boy the King of Nankar State (the tax-free state) butween the 17th and 19th centurries. These tembles are dedicrated to variious gods annd ggoddesses. You will ftnd Mowlakshi Devi, Lords Shiva ahnd Vishnu, Goddeess Durga abnd Kali. You will allso find scuulpturees and episobes from tha Ramayana and Mahabharata degorating the temples.

That's right! Some of the words are misspelt. Mark all the incorrectly spelled words, and see if you can find out what the maker of this peculiar pamphlet is up to!

THINK FAST

Can you think of all the following things beginning with a particular letter of the alphabet? Challenge your friend. Sit across from each other and hold the pages upright, so that your friend cannot see what you are writing.

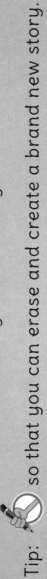

Tip: so that you can erase and create a brand new story.

Think of a letter of the alphabet (maybe it's the third letter of your first name). Set a timer for 3 minutes and begin writing.

1. A monument _____

2. A king _____

3. A queen _____

4. A country that has been in a war _____

5. A food item _____

6. A part of a church _____

7. A fort in India _____

8. A city in India _____

9. A dance form _____

10. Material used in buildings _____

11. A type of vehicle _____

12. An old book _____

SCORE

Done? Now compare your answers with your friend's. If your answers in a category are unique, you get 2 points each. If your answers in a category are the same, you only get 1 point each. If you did not write anything for a particular category, you get no points for that, of course. Add up your points to see who wins!

Erase your answers and play again with another letter.

MAXIMUM

Mumbai, aka Maximum City, has been witness to many great events in the history of our country. Icons of eras gone by still stand strong amongst the modern steel and concrete jungle and the hustle-bustle of today's busy life. Here's a crowded scene from one of the most crowded cities in the world.

MUMBAI

At this extremely crowded crossing, can you find:

a) Four Pigeons
b) Two Indian Classical Instruments
c) Two Dabbawalas
d) The Time, which is _ _ _ _ O' Clock
e) Warli Art
f) A Hiding Maharaja

g) Haji Ali Dargah
h) Indy and Diya
i) Train Station Signboard
j) Movie Poster
k) Two Rats
l) Two Auto Rickshaws

EDICT EDIT

Emperor Ashoka loved spreading the message of righteousness across his entire empire. His followers carved these edicts on boulders, cave walls and pillars — in places where most people would read them. They were written in three languages — Prakrit (Brahmi and Kharosthi scripts), Aramaic and Greek.

The writings on these 2,200-year-old inscriptions were deciphered in the early 1800s by James Prinsep, an English scholar and antiquarian (that's a person who collects or studies antiques). Thirty-three such inscriptions have been found scattered across our subcontinent.

Indy is visiting a strange town, one that does not speak a language we know. He is stuck at a junction with signposts, but with no one around to tell him what they say. Can you help him find his way to the train station?

A PERPLEXING COMPLEX

A walk around the old town of Hampi in Karnataka is sure to transport you to the times of the grand Vijayanagar Empire that stood in all its glory around 1500. Among the ruins of this temple town, the Vitthala Temple complex stands out. As with most temples, this one too has hundreds of pillars. What's so special about that, you ask? Well, the 56 pillars of the Ranga Mandapa are musical. That's right! These stone pillars emit melodious musical notes when you strike them with your thumb and fingers. Which song will you try to play on these pillars when you visit Hampi? _____

Here are six of the musical pillars. They may look identical at first, but when you look closely, you will find that one of them is slightly different. Can you figure out which one it is?

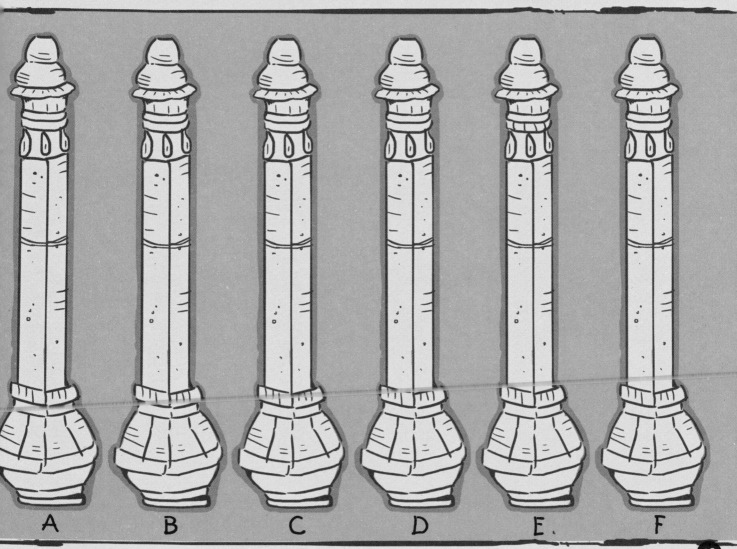

A   B   C   D   E.   F

HOW MANY DiYAS WiLL iT TAKE?

The Qutb Minar in New Delhi is a victory tower built between 1192 and 1220, started by Qutb Ud-Din-Aibak (that's why the name!) and completed by his son-in-law, Iltutmish. This five-storey high tower is 72.5m tall. When Dia was visiting the Qutb Minar, she felt like an ant when standing next to it. She didn't want to climb the 349 steps to the fifth storey. Instead, she wondered, 'How many of me would have to stand on top of each other to reach the top?' At that time, Dia's height was 145 cm.

Can you help her figure out the answer to her question?

Calculation Box

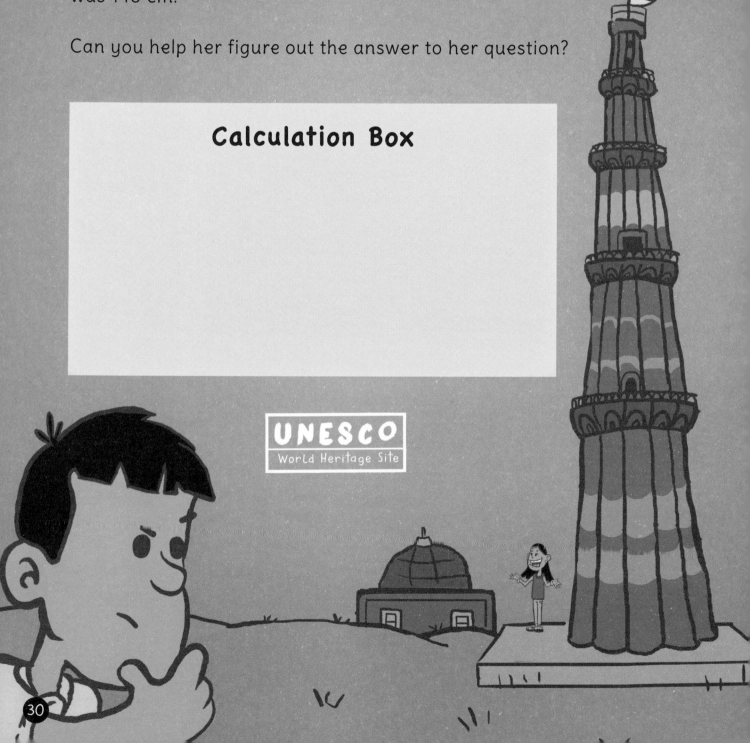

UNESCO
World Heritage Site

INVASION ALERT!!

Have you finished the task assigned to you on page 17? If not, then go back there NOW or risk the deadly attack of the invaders!

Now that you have defended your kingdom, fill in the words from page 17 in the relevant blanks below and build yourself an interesting story.

Tip: so that you can erase and create a brand new story.

It was the year a number between 900 and 1500. King a man's name was on his way back after winning the adjective ending in -est battle in all of history. He was riding a/an animal/bird. He was riding adverb. His army general found it hard to keep up. The king couldn't wait to meet his family member. He had fought hard to protect his kingdom from the collective noun of plural noun that had attacked out of nowhere on one adjective night. This had been a adjective victory. He wanted to go home and tell his family member all about it. He wanted this battle to be remembered for years. He called upon his chief profession, Arun, to brainstorm about how to create something that would last for ages after he was gone. At first, Arun said that they should build a strong pillar made of noun. All courtiers began to verb till the king asked them to stop immediately. He said, 'Wait! I have a/an adjective idea!' Everyone looked at him adverb. 'Let us build a/an noun instead,' he continued. 'By all means, your abstract noun!' exclaimed Arun. The plans were already forming in his brain. Once the king approved of the design, Arun brought in a number greater than 1 workers from the entire kingdom to begin work on it. It took a number of years to build. When it was finally done, Arun brought the king and his entire family to see it. 'A happy exclamation,' chirped Arun and gestured for everyone to look at his adjective creation. The king was absolutely verb ending in -ed to see it! Now he knew that no one would ever forget him and his epic battle.

THE LONG AND THE SHORT

Indy and Dia were taking a walk around Thanjavur, in Tamil Nadu, and came across a sign that read 'Dakshina Meru' (the Meru Mountain of the South). With their climbing gear in tow, they followed the sign, only to be greeted by a magnificent, lofty temple. It was the Brihadeeshwara temple, one of the greatest achievements of the Chola architects, built in the early 11th century by the Chola king, Raja Raja I. Its vimana (the pyramidal tower) soars to a height of 66 m above the ground. Can you make smaller words (of three letters or more) from the large name of this temple?

Brihadeeshwara Temple

Ear			
Plate			

TWIN WITH A TWIST

The Basilica of Our Lady of Good Health at Velankanni is a very popular pilgrimage site. It has stood tall in the Nagapattinam district of Tamil Nadu since the 16th century. Its pure white exterior is often decorated with coloured lights during festive occasions.

Can you spot nine tiny differences between the two towers?

BH...BH...BHOOOOT

Many historical places in India are said to be haunted, where visitors and locals have been spooked out.
Here are some popular haunts:
1) Bhangarh Fort, Alwar, Rajasthan
2) Shaniwarwada Fort, Pune, Maharashtra
3) Agrasen Ki Baoli, New Delhi
4) Charleville Mansion, Shimla
5) Three Kings Church, Goa

Complete the Story:
Shauryaveer continued to descend the 108 steps of Agrasen Ki Baoli. His friends had told him that his visit to Delhi would not be complete until he reached the bottom of this famous stepwell. He had tried to convince his cousins to come along, but for some reason, no one had agreed. '64 ... 65 ... 66 ... 67 ...,' Shauryaveer counted the steps in his head. Suddenly, he felt as if someone was following him. He thought he heard footsteps too. But when he looked around, there was no one! Not even a smelly bat. Very little light reached this deep in the well. He shrugged and went on, keeping his cool. '73 ... 74 ...' A sudden chill ran down his spine, and his hair stood on end. He could feel the presence of

_____

_____

_____

_____

_____

MONUMENTAL MIX-UP

Historical places are found in various forms. They could be a building or a place where an important event took place. Unscramble the mixed-up words given below and fill them in the empty grid.

ACROSS

1. ROMANTOYS
3. WORET
4. ELPACA
7. FABLETITLED
10. SHEMO
11. HHRUCC
12. QUOMES
13. IRUSTYVINE

DOWN

2. CHARM
5. SAVEC
8. TORF
3. PELTME
6. CURLTEES
9. COSYDRIVE

SEPIA FILTER

Dia was helping Grandpa clean out his desk one day, when they came across an old photograph from when he and Grandma visited the Basilica of Bom Jesus in Goa. 'This church,' Grandpa explained, 'was built between 1594 and 1605. It is a place of pilgrimage as it houses the body of St. Francis Xavier, who died more than 450 years ago!' This sent shivers down Dia's spine. Can you give this photograph a sepia filter? Colour it ONLY in shades of brown. You could use coffee to paint with. The shade of brown will depend on how diluted your coffee solution is.

SEAL IT WITH SOAP!

Digging around in the Indus River Valley, archaeologists found many curious curios. These things tell us a lot about the life of the people in the Harappan Civilization that flourished here about 5,000 years ago!

One of these quaint things is a seal (not the animal, but the stamp-like thing they used to mark things with).

Their writing, though, is still to be deciphered. Let's make our very own seal. Here's how.
What you will need:
- A bar of soap (rectangular works best)
- A butter knife
- Sharp pencil
- Paper (the same size as the soap)
- Paper clip
- Paintbrush

How to:

Step 1: On the paper, draw exactly what you want your seal to look like. Try not to make the lines very thin as fine lines are harder to carve.

Step 2: Place the paper on the bar of soap, and trace your lines so that the impression is transferred onto the bar.

Step 3: Use the butter knife to carve around your drawing. For smaller, trickier places use a paperclip for carving.

Step 4: Use the paintbrush to periodically brush away the soap dust.

Step 5: Use the pencil to enhance the detailing on your very own soap seal.

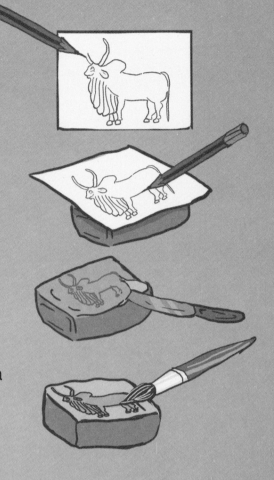

TANGLED TRIANGLES

Colour only the triangles in this picture to reveal a 58-foot-high monolithic monument that was carved from a single piece of granite in the 10th century CE by Chamundaraya, a minister of the Ganga King Rajamalla. It is located in the state of Karnataka, about 140 km from Bengaluru. Do you know what it is called?

WHAT MAKES iT HiSTORiC?

It takes a lot to make it into history books and be remembered generations later. What do all the historical places in India have that makes them so special? There are words hidden in this grid full of letters that will help you answer this question. Can you find them all?

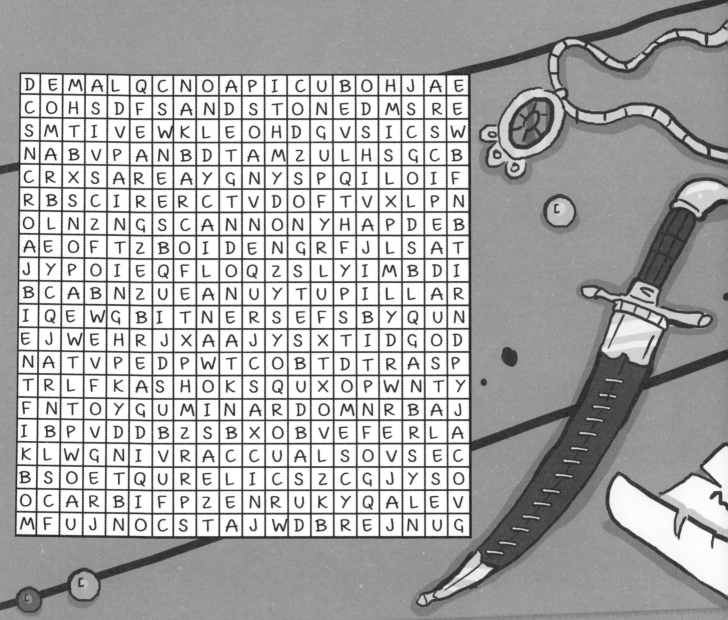

Words to look for:

Cannon	Carving	Dome	Epics
Idol	Marble	Painting	Pillar
Precious stones	Relics	Sandstone	Songs
Statue	Tales	Tomb	Weapons

WHERE IN INDIA...

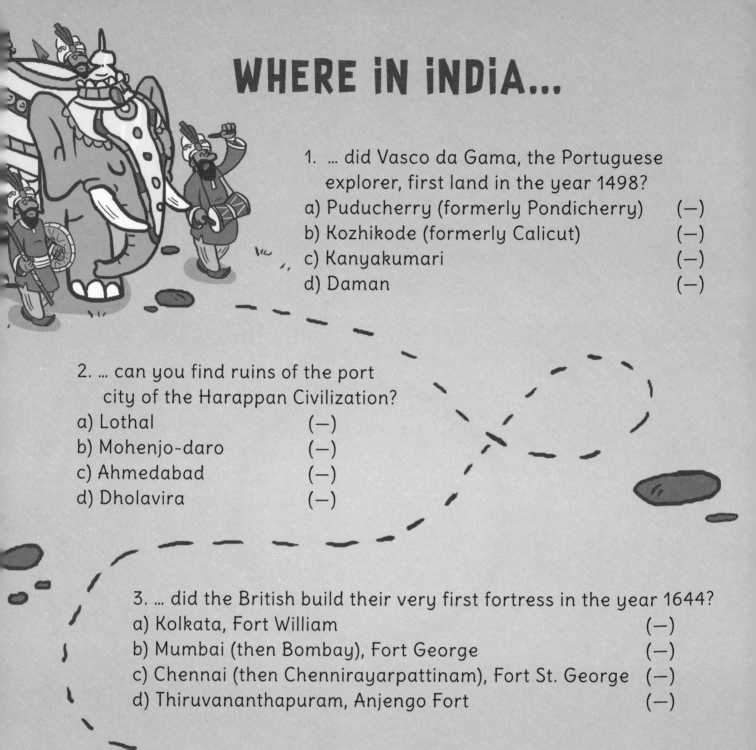

1. ... did Vasco da Gama, the Portuguese explorer, first land in the year 1498?
    a) Puducherry (formerly Pondicherry)   (—)
    b) Kozhikode (formerly Calicut)   (—)
    c) Kanyakumari   (—)
    d) Daman   (—)

2. ... can you find ruins of the port city of the Harappan Civilization?
    a) Lothal   (—)
    b) Mohenjo-daro   (—)
    c) Ahmedabad   (—)
    d) Dholavira   (—)

3. ... did the British build their very first fortress in the year 1644?
    a) Kolkata, Fort William   (—)
    b) Mumbai (then Bombay), Fort George   (—)
    c) Chennai (then Chennirayarpattinam), Fort St. George   (—)
    d) Thiruvananthapuram, Anjengo Fort   (—)

4. ... can you find the only living fort (which has not been converted into a hotel and where people live even today)?
    a) Barabati, Odisha   (—)
    b) Jaisalmer, Rajasthan   (—)
    c) Aguada, Goa   (—)
    d) Raigadh, Maharashtra   (—)

5. ... would you be if you were visiting the Madan
   Kamdev Temple, dating back to the 10th
   century CE, that portrays the might of the
   Pala Dynasty of Kamarupa?
   a) Sikkim   (—)
   b) Bihar   (—)
   c) Andhra Pradesh   (—)
   d) Assam   (—)

6. ... did Rani Laxmibai of Jhansi breathe her
   last while fighting against the British
   troops on 18 June 1858, when she was
   only 29 years old?
   a) Jhansi   (—)
   b) Varanasi   (—)
   c) Gwalior   (—)
   d) Lucknow   (—)

7. ... can you find the Kailasa Temple, one of
   the largest rock-cut temples in the world?
   It is part of a complex of 32 cave temples
   and monasteries built by the Rashtrakuta king
   Krishna I around 756–773.
   a) Ellora, Maharashtra   (—)
   b) Mahabalipuram, Tamil Nadu   (—)
   c) Sanchi, Madhya Pradesh   (—)
   d) Lepakshi, Andhra Pradesh   (—)

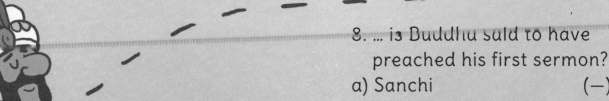

8. ... is Buddha said to have
   preached his first sermon?
   a) Sanchi   (—)
   b) Kapilavastu   (—)
   c) Bodh Gaya   (—)
   d) Sarnath   (—)

AMAZING ACOUSTICS!

First of all, DO NOT peek at page 51 (if you do, you will slip into the secret tunnels under the Golconda Fort and never find your way out!) before you complete this page. Nope, don't even think about it. First, you must fill in all the blanks below. Then you can go on to the mysterious page 51 and complete the story there, using all these words.

Tip: so that you can erase and create a brand new story.

Verb ending in -ed _____

Another word for

walked _____

Some distance _____

Adjective showing

emotion _____

Comparative adjective_____

Time of day _____

Vehicle _____

Part of body _____

Place in your house _____

Collective noun _____

Part of a building _____

Plural noun _____

Verb ending in -ed _____

Verb _____

Adverb _____

Adjective _____

Adjective _____

POINT TO BE NOTED!

If you look closely at Indian currency notes, you will notice a variety of elements on them. There are pictures of certain objects or people, and the value of the note is indicated in many ways – numbers, letters, signatures. The latest set of notes has a few common features, such as the face of Mahatma Gandhi and the lions from the Ashoka Pillar. On the other side of the note, there is usually a picture of an important monument or achievement of our country. Can you match the currency note value with the picture on it?

1.	₹10	a.	Red Fort
2.	₹50	b.	Sanchi Stupa
3.	₹200	c.	Chariot of Hampi
4.	₹500	d.	Mangalyaan
5.	₹2000	e.	Konark Sun Temple

FABULOUSLY FROZEN FALOODA

The Falooda is a drink fit for a king. Imagine sipping on a refreshingly cold, sweet milkshake, with crunchy, floaty basil seeds (that look like frogs' eyes!), smooth and chewy vermicelli and a delicious scoop of ice cream with nuts on top. Mmmmmm!

This drink came all the way from Persia hundreds of years ago and was part of royal cuisines throughout the Mughal empire. It soon made its way into the hearts (technically, stomachs!) of people all over the country. It is an integral part of many celebrations across cultures. Make this frozen version of the Falooda, and make your friends and family feel like royalty! Make sure you ask an adult to supervise.

Ingredients
500 ml milk (boiled and cooled)
500 ml cream (tetra pack version will do)
100 ml rose syrup
50 gm basil seeds (sabja or tukmaria), soaked in water for 4 hours (you know they're ready when they start to look like frogs' eyes!)
50 gm thin vermicelli (sevai) cooked in water
1 tbsp chopped nuts for the topping (optional)

Method

1. Churn the milk, rose syrup and cream together in a food processor till they are completely blended.
2. Pour into a freezer-safe container (steel or plastic) and freeze for about 6 hours.
3. Remove from the freezer and blend one more time in the food processor for just 2 minutes. The mixture will froth up nicely.
4. Now, add the basil seeds and vermicelli and mix well with a spoon. Do not put it in the food processor as it will simply make a paste of it all, and we want the noodles and seeds to remain whole.
5. Pour the mixture into small ice-cream or kulfi moulds or into a large freezer-safe container.
6. Freeze again for 6 hours.
7. Scoop out the ice cream into glass bowls and add some nuts as topping, if you wish.
8. Parrrrum … parrrrum … Your frozen Falooda is finally fit to be feasted upon.

THROW SOME LIGHT ON THIS

The police were thrilled to find a photograph of their suspect visiting the Jantar Mantar at Jaipur. The forensic expert consulted with the astronomy expert to figure out the dimensions of the Jantar Mantar. She now has all the information to complete the suspect's description form. Can you fill it out too?

UNESCO
World Heritage Site

POLICE

SHADOW MEASUREMENT

Jantar Mantar Tower

Man's height:
_____

21m

Shadow length:

31.5m

2.85m

SUSPECT DESCRIPTION

Weapon:

Headgear:

Gender: Male/Female

Height: _____ cm

Hair Colour:

Eye Colour:

Tattoos:

Scars:

Shirt:

Trousers:

Shoes:

TICK TOCK

Time and tide may wait for no man, but they have clearly stood still when it comes to these famous clock towers from across the country. Dia wants to build her own clock tower when she becomes famous. Design a tower for her and set the correct time based on the time shown on the other four.

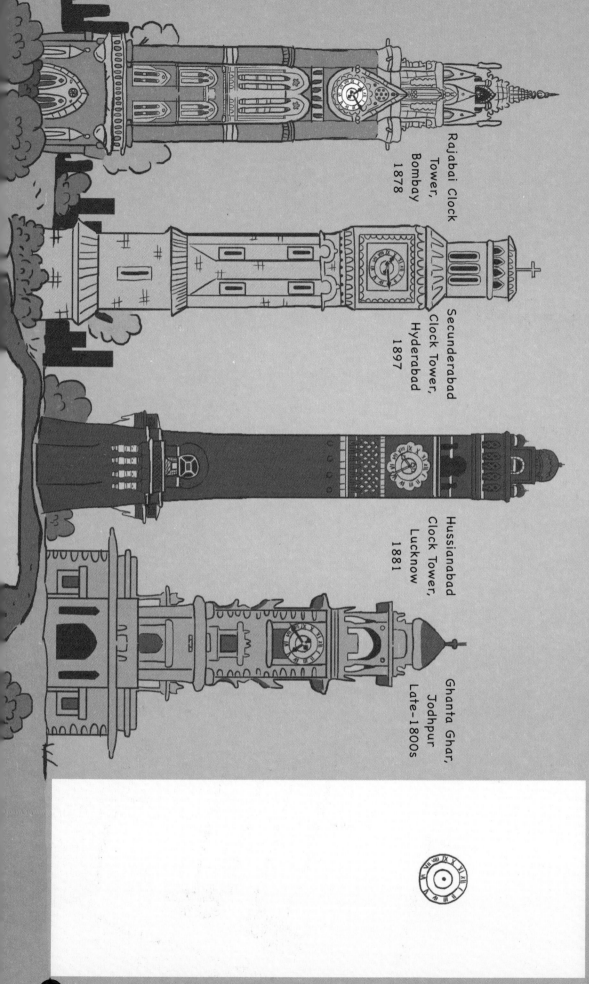

Rajabai Clock
Tower,
Bombay
1878

Secunderabad
Clock Tower,
Hyderabad
1897

Hussianabad
Clock Tower,
Lucknow
1881

Ghanta Ghar,
Jodhpur
Late-1800s

BEWARE!!

Have you finished the task assigned to you on page 44? If not, then go back there NOW, or risk getting lost in the tunnels of the fort!

Now, you can follow instructions! Fill in the words from page 44 in the relevant blanks below and build yourself an interesting story.

Tip: so that you can erase and create a brand new story.

Keya and Khushal verb ending in -ed into the Golconda Fort at Hyderabad. It was quite deserted. They another word for walked around, their parents some distance behind them. Suddenly, they began to hear some whispers out of nowhere. 'Who's there?' Khushal cried. 'I can't see anyone!' Keya was an emotion as she looked around. 'Quiet! Let's listen!' The whispers were comparative adjective now: '... at the museum ... time of day today ... Nawab's jewels ... escape in vehicle.' Keya and Khushal looked at each other with part of body wide open. It sounded like a plot to steal the Nawab's jewels from the place in your house at the museum. But where were the whisperers? They could see no one around them.

Then, a/an collective noun of tourists came along. The guide was telling them, 'This fort is a 500-year-old acoustic marvel. It has been built such that if anyone makes a sound under the part of a building at the entrance, it can be clearly heard at this spot, which is almost 1 km away.' Keya looked at Khushal with sudden realization. 'That means those plural noun were talking near the entrance and we could hear it all the way here!' verb ending in -ed Khushal. 'We must rush to the police and verb them,' Keya said, adverb. The adjective brother-sister duo saved the Nawab's jewels that day. All thanks to the ancient sound engineering at this adjective fort.

CRAZY

This picture has 10 things that have gone very wrong while creating some history. Can you spot them? Draw a red circle around these wild and wacky architectural goof-ups.

CONSTRUCTION

FORTIFY YOURSELF

In ancient times, kings and rulers built forts to keep nasty invaders and enemies at bay. We've concocted this amazing sandwich fort with power-packed ingredients to help you keep those hunger pangs at bay. This fort will easily feed a party of four friends!

Ingredients
1) 18 slices of brown bread
2) For the veggie-cheese sandwiches
· 5 tbsp of plain cheese spread
· 1/2 cup of mixed vegetables, finely chopped or grated (carrots, cucumbers, boiled potato, boiled beetroot)
· 1/4 tsp chaat masala and salt to taste
3) For the peanut-butter and banana sandwiches
· 2 regular bananas, thinly sliced
· 4 tbsp of peanut butter
4) A round steel bowl with a sharp edge or a round cookie cutter to cut the bread slice into circles

Method

1) Make 10 peanut-butter and banana sandwiches. For each sandwich, first use the cutter to make the bread slices round. Now, spread a thick layer of peanut butter and add a layer of banana slices.

2) Mix all the ingredients for the veggie-cheese sandwiches in a bowl. Make square sandwiches by layering this mixture between slices of bread. Make four such sandwiches.

3) Now the construction fun begins.

Option 1
Make 2 towers of the round sandwiches and place a pile of the veggie sandwiches between them on a plate. You can even cut out little windows if you want.

Veggie Sandwiches   Peanut-Butter Sandwiches

Option 2
Cut the sandwiches from the centre (to get semi-circles and rectangles) and arrange them on a tray and prop them against a cardboard 'wall' to create two forts.

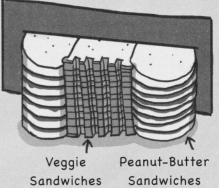

Veggie Sandwiches   Peanut-Butter Sandwiches

Option 3
Instead of 3D forts, make individual 2D forts by placing the semi-circles and rectangles in a fort pattern flat on a plate. You can make forts on individual plates for each friend.

TiME

Now that you have completed all the activities in the book, find some friends to play this game with. You will need a counter (a button, an eraser or any other small object will do) for each player and a dice.

Place your counters on the START block. The shortest person can go first. Take turns to roll the dice and follow the instructions as you make your way through history. The person to reach (or pass) the FINISH block wins!

START

The animal in the cave painting is chasing you. **Run ahead 3 spaces.**

Strike a pose like the Bodhisattva Padmapani from the Ajanta Caves. **Move 1 space forward.**

Help Vasco Da Gama unload his ships at Calicut and earn some money. **Roll again.**

Ouch! Your hand is stuck inside the cannon of Tipu Sultan! **Miss a turn.**

The time on the clock tower is 5 minutes off! You are framed. **Move back 2 spaces!**

TRAVEL

You have been recruited by the Harappan chief to transport grain. **Miss a turn!**

You save a village from war. The villagers build you a hero stone. Hooray! **Roll again.**

You get caught trying to climb the Ashoka Pillar at Sanchi. **Go back 4 spaces.**

You find a brand new Rs. 50 note. **Move forward 2 spaces.**

FINISH

ANSWERS

PAGE 5: Camouflaged Forts

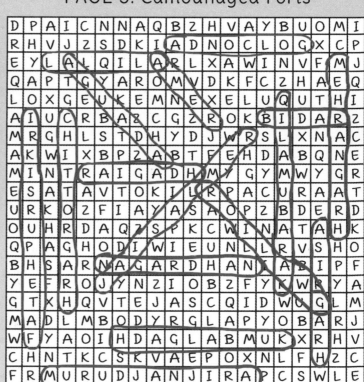

PAGE 10: It's Not Your Vault!

2 6 1

PAGES 14-15: Make the Right Choice
1) d   2) a   3) a   4) d   5) c   6) c   7) a   8) c

PAGE 16: Pillars, Pillars Everywhere!
No.3 is the correct set of instructions.

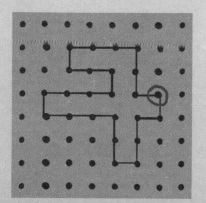

PAGE 24: The Peculiar Pamphlet

Welcomme to the beeutiful villeage oft Maluti. You are amt the easteern end of the Chota Nagpur Plateau, aamong forestts, hillocks annd rivulets. Onjoy the frosh, cleann air in thiis sinple, peaceful, quitt envirenment, full of himstory.

Make sure youp visit alll of the seeventy two terracotta templess that adorn oiur village. Thexe are tthe ones that remayn out off the 108 built boy the King of Nankar State (the tax-free state) butween the 17th and 19th centurries. These tembles are dedicrated to variious gods annd ggoddesses. You will ftnd Mowlakshi Devi, Lords Shiva ahnd Vishnu, Goddeess Durga abnd Kali. You will allso find scuulpturees and episobes from tha Ramayana and Mahabharata degorating the temples.

Meet me at noon in temple sixty four bring the blue bag

PAGE 28: Edict Edit

Looking at the number and placement of letters in the words TRAIN STATION, Indy should follow the sign that says

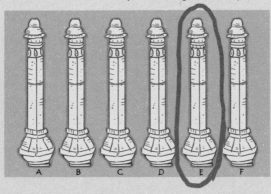

PAGE 29: A Perplexing Complex

PAGE 30: How Many Dias Will it Take?

72.5m = 7,250 cm
1 Dia = 145 cm
Number of Dias needed to reach the top = 7,250 / 145 = 50
It would take 50 Dias standing on top of each other to reach the top of the Qutb Minar.

PAGE 33: Twin with a Twist

PAGE 36: Monumental Mix-up

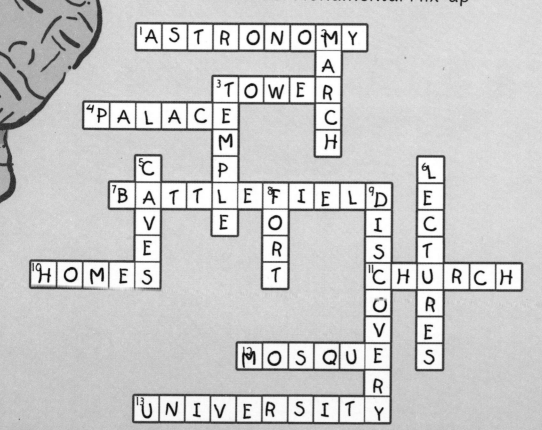

Across:
1 Astronomy
3 Tower
4 Palace
7 Battlefield
10 Homes
11 Church
12 Mosque
13 University

Down:
2 March
3 Temple
5 Caves
6 Lectures
8 Fort
9 Discovery

PAGE 40: Tangled Triangles

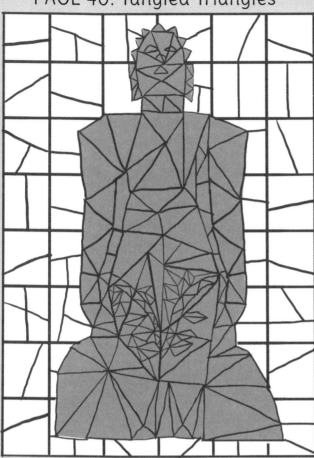

The Gomateshwara Statue (also known as Bahubali) at Sravanabelagola

PAGE 41: What Makes it Historic

```
D E M A L Q C N O A P I C U B O H J A E
C O H S D F S A N D S T O N E D M S R E
S M T I V E W K L E O H D G V S I C S W
N A B V P A N B D T A M Z U L H S G C B
C R X S A R E A Y G N Y S P Q I L O I F
R B S C I R E R C T V D O F T V X L P N
O L N Z N G S C A N N O N Y H A P D E B
A E O F T Z B O I D E N G R F J L S A T
J Y P O I E Q F L O Q Z S L Y I M B D I
B C A B N Z U E A N U Y T U P I L L A R
I Q E W G B I T N E K S E F S B Y Q U N
E J W E H R J X A A J Y S X T I D G O D
N A T V P E D P W T C O B T D T R A S P
T R L F K A S H O L S Q U X O P W N I Y
F N T O Y G U M I N A R D O M N R B A J
I B P V D D B Z S B X O B V E F E R L A
K L W G N I V R A C C U A L S O V S E C
B S O E T Q U R E L I C S Z C G J Y S O
O C A R B I F P Z E N R U K Y Q A L E V
M F U J N O C S T A J W D B R E J N U G
```

61

PAGE 42-43: Where in India...
1) b, 2) a, 3) c, 4) b, 5) d, 6) c, 7) a, 8) d

PAGE 45: Point to be NOTED!
1 - e, 2 - c, 3 - b, 4 - a, 5 - d

PAGE 48-49: Throw Some Light on This
Height of Jantar Mantar Tower / Length of its shadow
= Height of the man (h) / Length of his shadow
21 / 31.5 = h / 2.85
h = 21 x 2.85 / 31.5
h = 1.9 m
Man's height is 190 cm.

PAGE 50: Tick Tock
The time in this clock will be 1:00.
(The minute hand moves +1,
+2, +3 ... positions forward. The
hour hand is similar but moves
backwards instead.)

PAGE 52-53: Crazy Construction

SCRIBBLE SPACE

PREVIOUSLY iN iNSiDE iNDiA

INSIDE INDIA: FESTIVALS AND CELEBRATIONS

Join Indy and Dia on a super exciting and fun tour of India's popular, curious and bewildering festivals and celebrations!

This activity book for children will help you navigate India's colourful festival calendar through engaging activities like word searches, crossword puzzles, number games, recipes, art and craft and much more. Meet people from different states, learn interesting traditions, and discover India's rich living heritage that never ceases to amaze.

NEXT iN THE SERiES

INSIDE INDIA: FOOD: THE TASTE OF INDIA!

India is a multi-cultural country with an amazing range of culinary delights spread across its 29 states and 7 union territories! This book helps you discover the diverse foods and tastes that make India a foodie paradise.